33 Reasons Why I Love My Dad!

Written by A'miyah Griffith
Illustrated by Nate Sheridan

I love my dad because...

he helps me with my reading.

he buys me clothes.

he bought me a laptop.

he cooks me breakfast.

I love my dad because...

he is smart.

he bought me a bike.

he takes me to school.

he picks me up from school.

I love my dad because...
he makes me laugh.

I love my dad because...

he buys birthday presents.

he helps me with my maths.

he let me have sleepovers.

he bought me a phone.

I love my dad because...

he drives me to my destinations.

I love my dad because...

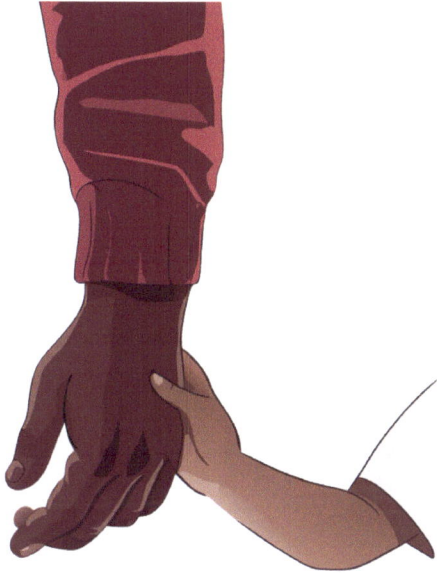

he cares about me.

he bought me headphones.

he lets me have sweets.

he bought me a watch.

I love my dad because...
he makes me things.

I love my dad because...

he takes care of me when I'm sick.

he bought me a camera.

he buys me toys.

he lets me have takeout.

I love my dad because...

he does arts and crafts with me.

I love my dad because...

he lets me eat crisps.

he cooks me dinner.

he buys me Christmas presents.

I love my dad because...
he takes me to the park.

I love my dad because...

he bought me a tablet.

he takes me to church.

he takes me to the doctor if I am sick.

he bought me a scooter.

Mostly, I love my dad because
he loves me!

www.ingramcontent.com/pod-product-compliance
Lightning Source LLC
Chambersburg PA
CBHW042108040426

42448CB00002B/181